Street Art

By Jill Atkins

Published in 2026 by
Norwood House Press
2544 Clinton Street
Buffalo, NY 14224

Printed in the United States of America

Library of Congress Cataloging-in-Publication Data:
Names: Atkins, Jill (Children's author). | Jones, Cath, 1965-, author. | Rowland, Ceej, illustrator.
Title: Street art / written by Jill Atkins. The deal / written by Cath Jones, illustrated by Ceej Rowland. A week in the Sahara / written by Jill Atkins.
Description: Buffalo, NY : Norwood House Press, 2026. | Series: Phonics all-stars: phase 5a
Identifiers: ISBN 9781978578920 (pbk.) | ISBN 9781978578937 (library bound) | ISBN 9781978578944 (ebook)
Subjects: LCSH: Reading–Phonetic method–Juvenile fiction. | English language–Phonetics–Juvenile fiction. | Street art–Juvenile fiction. | Graffiti–Juvenile fiction. | Music–Juvenile fiction. | Bands (Music)–Juvenile fiction. | Sahara–Juvenile fiction.
Classification: LCC LB1573.3 A796 2026 | DDC 372.465–dc23

CPSIA compliance information: Batch #CW26NHP: For further information contact Norwood House Press at 1-800-237-9932.

If you are out and about, you might see some street art.

Good street artists have a lot of skill.

There are all sorts of street art.

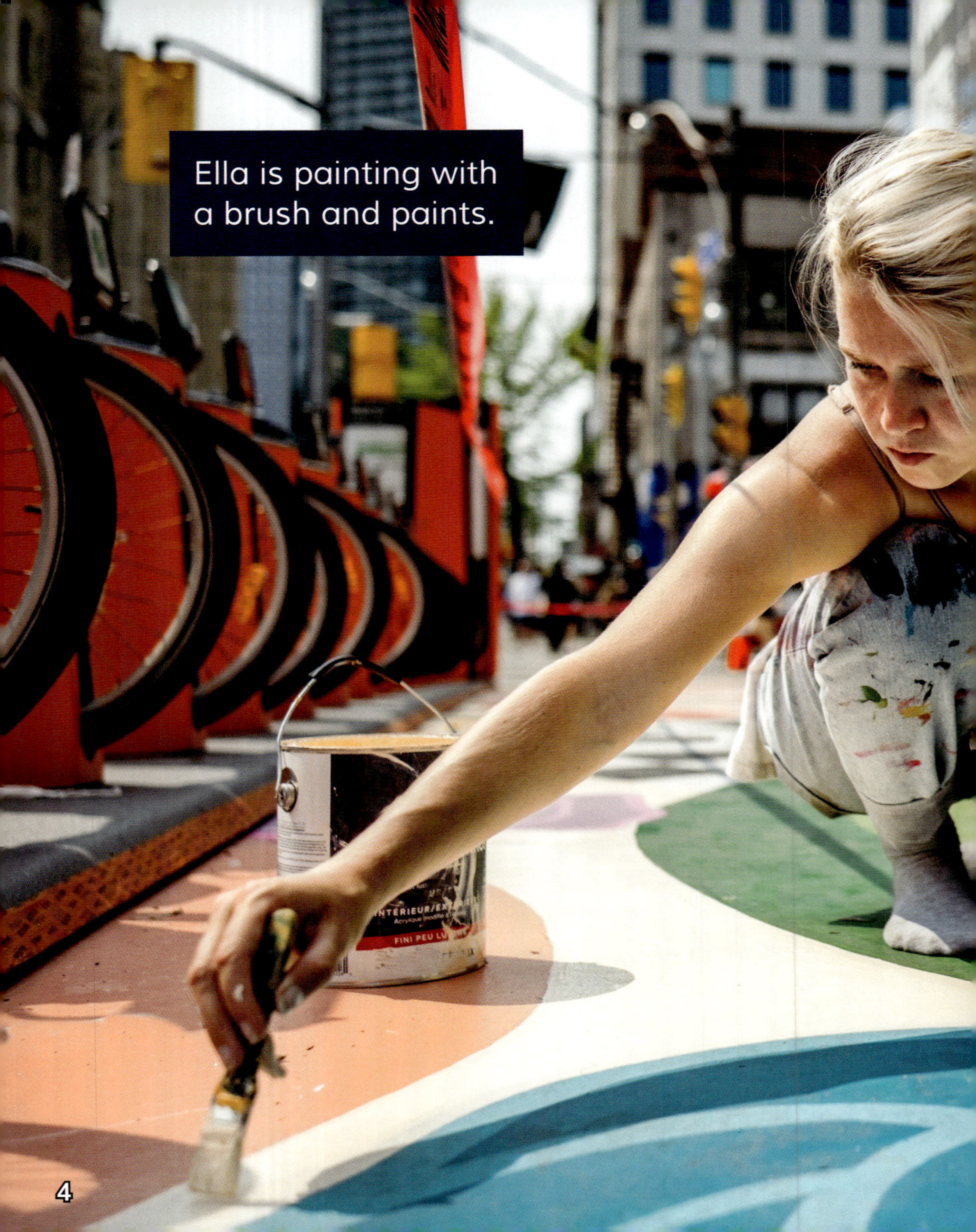

Ella is painting with a brush and paints.

Mai is painting
with a spray can.

Is this street art?

I think so. It is fun and will brighten her day. She is glad it is there.

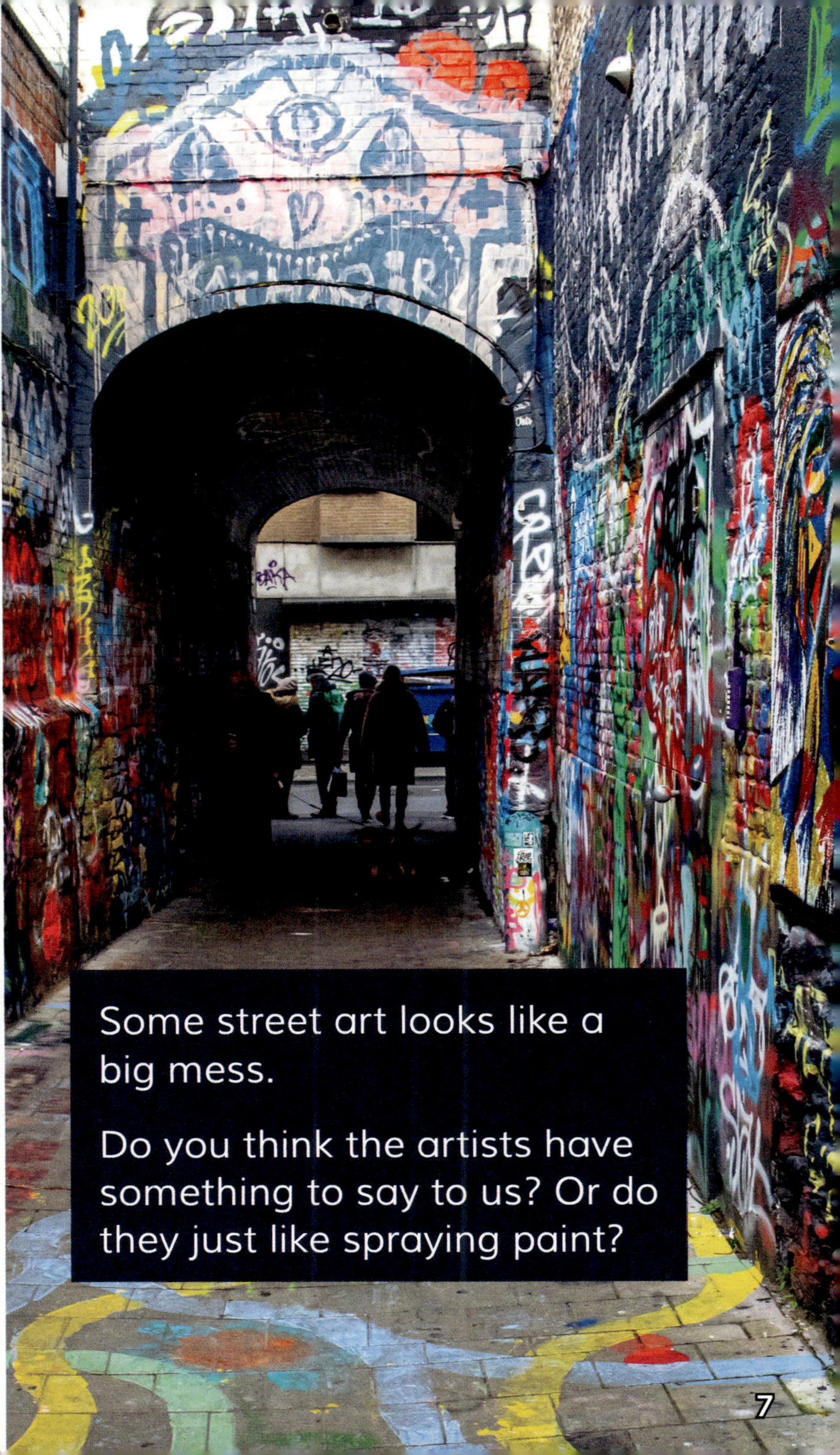

Some street art looks like a big mess.

Do you think the artists have something to say to us? Or do they just like spraying paint?

Is this art?
That is not art.
This is art!
I think
it is art.
What is art?

Some street art will stay forever, but some is not so good. It will need to go.

Del is painting on top of the bad art.

Look at this tunnel.

That must have been a big job. I bet it took countless weeks to finish it.

Do you like this archway?

Do you think the artist has talent?

Some street art is little. This isn't!

Anna May is painting trees. She is standing on a ladder so she can paint the tops of the trees.

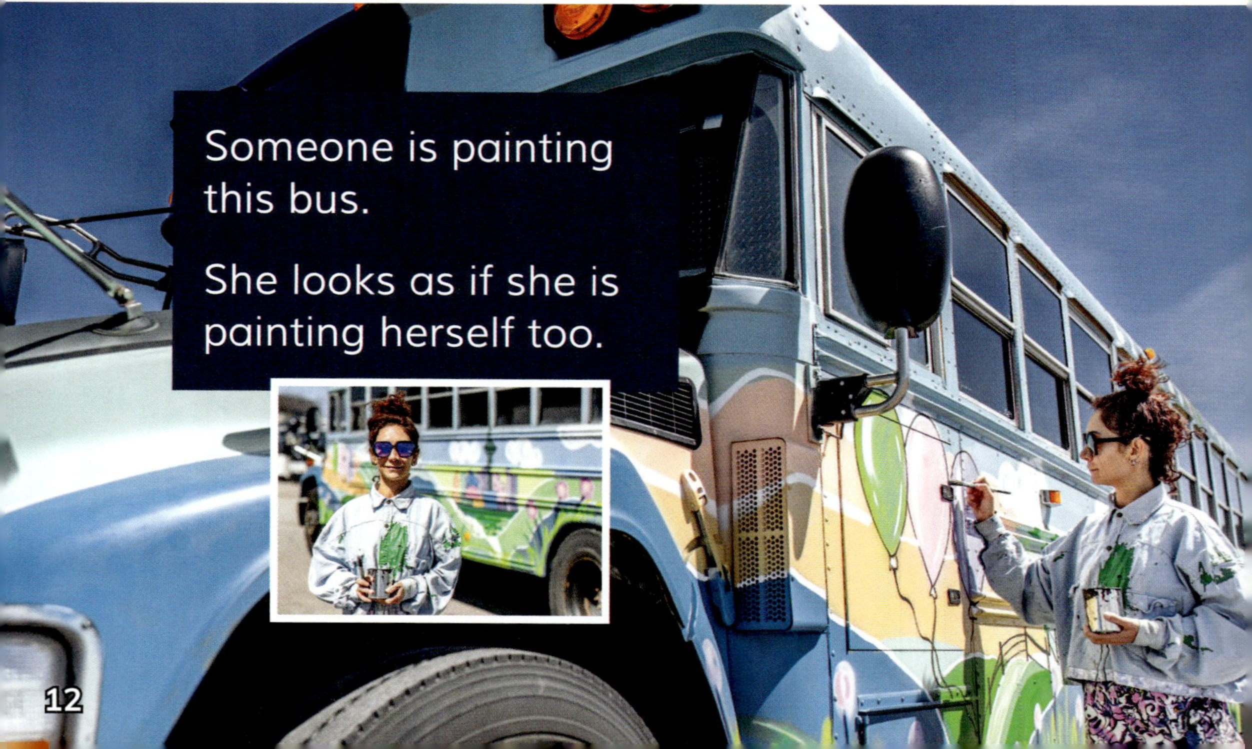

Someone is painting this bus.

She looks as if she is painting herself too.

You might see some street art on a trolley car, like this.

Look at this. What can you see? Do you think you might drop into the big gap?

No! The art is all on the ground. There is no gap to drop into.

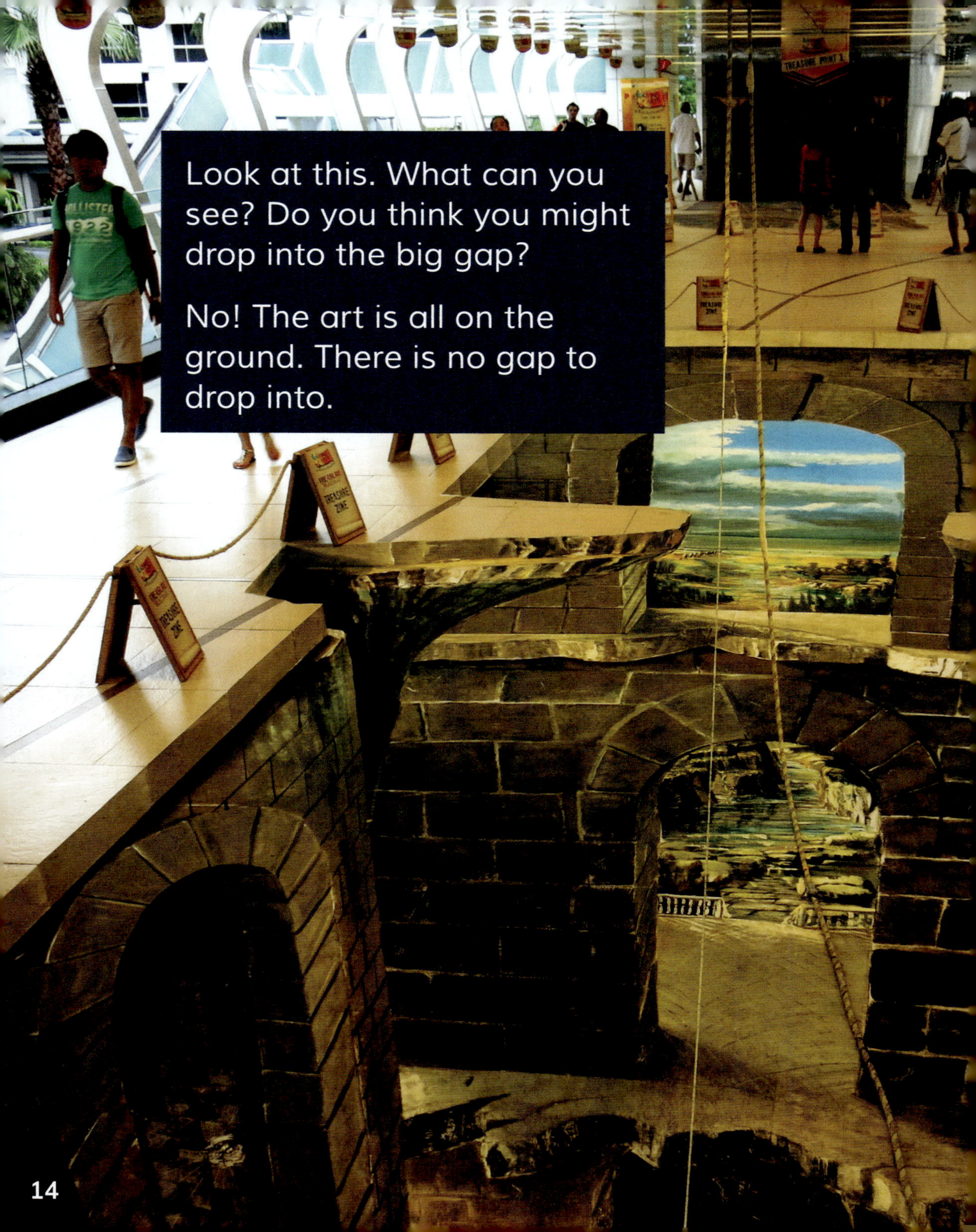

Some kids like to play
with crayons in the street.

They do it just for fun.
If it rains, the art will go.

But
I still say it's
not art.

The Deal

Written by
Cath Jones

Illustrated by
Ceej Rowland

Fran picked up her trumpet. Next to her, Krishnan was seated with his drum. They were waiting for Max's signal.

Max held up his hand and yelled, "1-2, 1-2-3-4!"

Fran grinned as she tried to keep up with Krishnan's quick drum beat.

Max was a thrilling rapper. It was a big treat to be in a band as good as this.

The next morning, Max strutted into the room.

"We have got a booking!" he said.

Fran was astonished.

"The man running that run-down little club in Dock Street said we can be the opening band – this weekend."

"Oh wow!" Krishnan punched the air.

Fran beamed. They'd had a long wait for something like this.

That weekend, Max, Fran, and Krishnan met on Dock Street.

The club was in darkness. There was a big padlock too.

“Something’s up, Krish,” said Fran with a sinking feeling.

“It looks like the club has shut down,” Max added.

He was right. Their gig was off.

"Let's go," said Fran. "There's no point standing in this dark street."

Krishnan was fed up.
"We'll have to get the bus back," he said.

There was a crowd waiting at the bus stop.

“I think all the buses have vanished into thin air!” a man in the crowd said. “We might have a long wait.”

All of a sudden, Krishnan started tapping his drum. Then Max started to rap.

Fran got out her trumpet.

"We might as well be a band for the crowd," she said as she joined in. As well as her trumpet, Fran started to rap too.

Then a man waiting for a bus stepped up to the three band members. He was tapping his feet to the beat.

When Krishnan, Max, and Fran stopped, the man took out a card and handed it to Fran.

"I think I can offer you a deal," he said. "Let's do some songs and see."

Fran beamed. "You like the band?"

"I like **you**," he said. "Trumpet and rap – that's a compelling mix!"

"What happens to the rest of the band?" Fran said. "Max ... and Krish?"

"Just you," he said. "**You're** going to be a star."

Fran shifted to look at Krishnan and Max.

"Just you," the man had said. That was the deal.

What was she going to do?

A Week in the Sahara

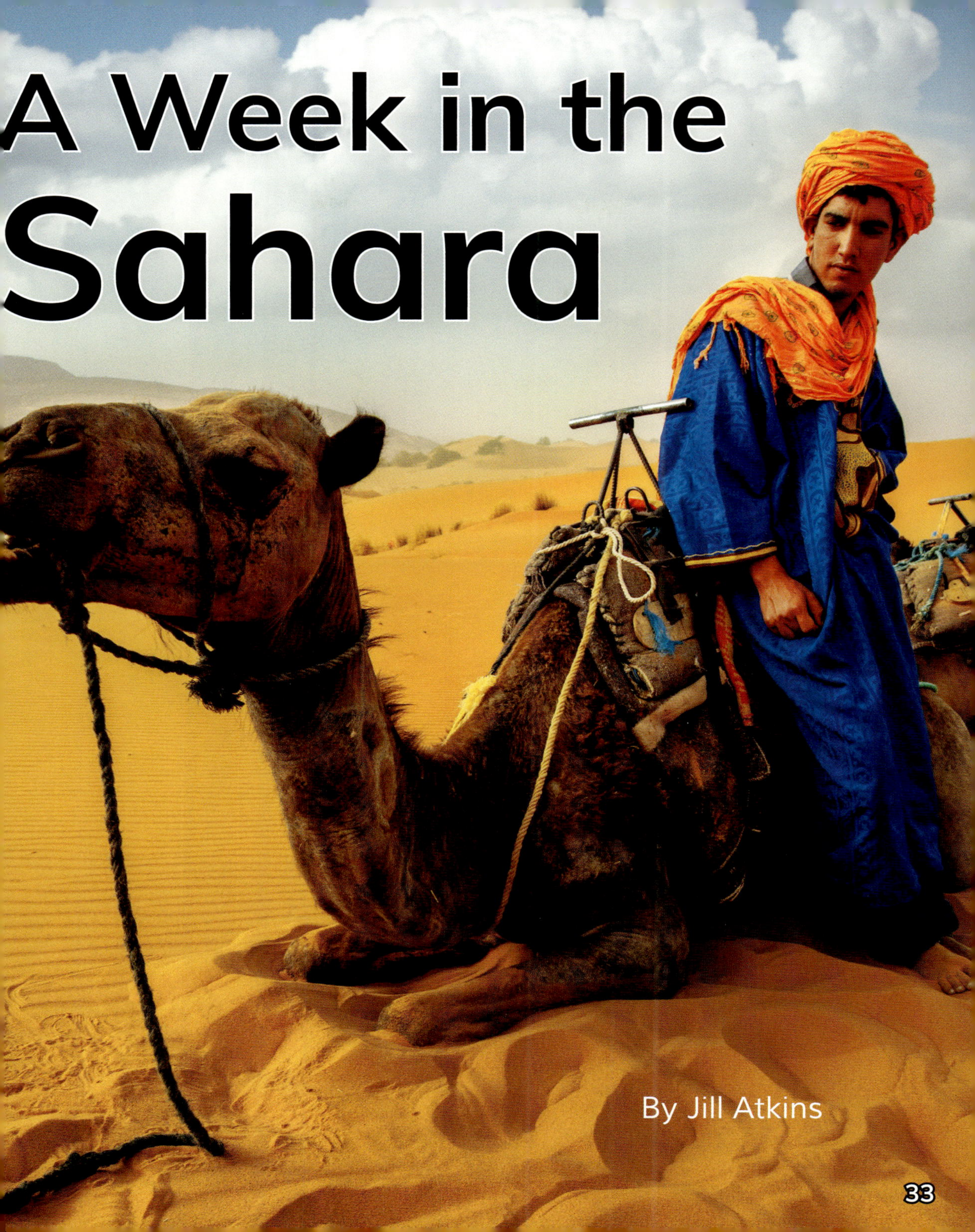

By Jill Atkins

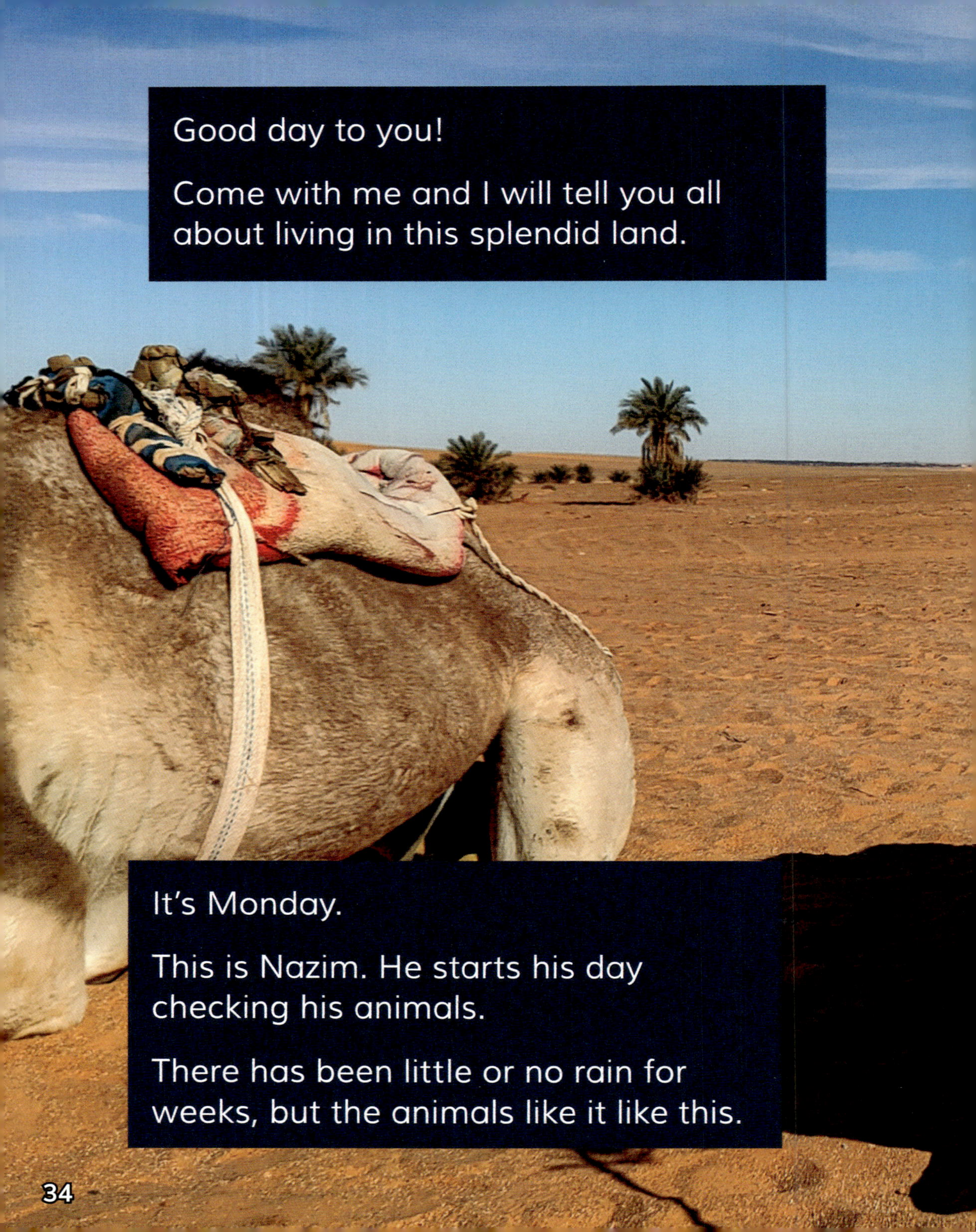

Good day to you!

Come with me and I will tell you all about living in this splendid land.

It's Monday.

This is Nazim. He starts his day checking his animals.

There has been little or no rain for weeks, but the animals like it like this.

Now it's Tuesday.

Some men go out with their goats.

The goats are important, as the men get milk and meat from them.

Oh, how packed with cream and goodness that milk is! (The meat is good too.)

On Wednesday morning, Yanis picks out his best goats.

He brings them back, near his hamlet.

The goats rest in the hot sun. They will stay there for the night.

The next day, Thursday, Farid brings his goats to market.

Farid needs to sell his goats for cash.

Or he might barter a goat for some tools.

On Friday, Asma and Hana go to the food market in the next town.

Asma is looking for some peppermint and some radishes. She needs the best deal.

Hana might select some beans, cooking oil, and meat.

Oh, and I forgot – some groundnuts too.

It's Saturday – a big day for cooking.

Hamed is cooking chicken. This is the way we cook it in the Sahara.

He needs some hot tea too.

They cannot have their chicken without tea to drink with it!

It's Sunday – the day our animals get to rest. For us, they are our pickup trucks. We must keep them well.

Hamza must tie them up, or they will run off.

Will you pay a visit to the Sahara one day?